seafood

seafood

delicious ideas for salads, soups, pasta, and more

RYLAND
PETERS
& SMALL

LONDON NEW YORK

First published in the United States in 2006
by Ryland Peters & Small, Inc.
519 Broadway, 5th Floor, New York, NY 10012
www.rylandpeters.com

10 9 8 7 6 5 4 3 2 1

Library of Congress Cataloging-in-Publication Data

Seafood : delicious ideas for salads, soups, pasta, and
more / Julz Beresford ... [et al.].
     p. cm.
  Includes index.
  ISBN-13: 978-1-84597-128-1
  ISBN-10: 1-84597-128-0
  1. Cookery (Seafood) 2. Cookery, International. I.
Beresford, Julz.
  TX747.S366 2006
  641.6'92–dc22

                                        2005028557

Printed in China

Designer Luana Gobbo

Editor Sharon Cochrane

Picture Research Emily Westlake

Production Paul Harding

Editorial Director Julia Charles

Art Director Anne-Marie Bulat

Publishing Director Alison Starling

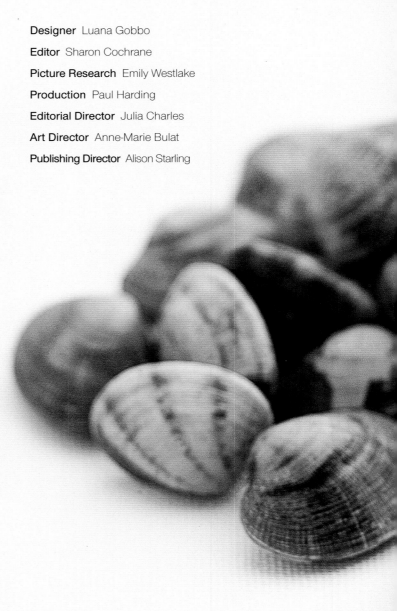

Notes
• All spoon measurements are level unless otherwise
specified.
• All eggs are large unless otherwise specified.
Uncooked or partly cooked eggs should not be served
to the very young, the very old, those with compromised
immune systems, or to pregnant women.

contents

introduction

Seafood is wonderfully versatile—it can be used in soups and salads, risottos and pasta dishes, salads and tarts, or simply on its own. From Southeast Asia to the Mediterranean, seafood is used in many different and delicious ways.

Seafood is easy to prepare, so don't be afraid to cook it at home. Just ensure you follow a few simple guidelines. Always buy seafood from a reputable source and when it is as fresh as possible—choose whatever looks the freshest and best on the day. Store it in the refrigerator until needed, and eat it preferably on the day of purchase. If you are using frozen seafood, ensure that it is thoroughly thawed in the refrigerator before cooking. Shellfish should be alive when you buy it fresh and raw. Check any open mussels or clams by tapping them against a hard surface; they should close when you do so, discard any that stay open.

It is easy to overcook seafood, so watch it carefully while it is cooking and follow the timings in the recipes closely. If it is cooked too long, it will be tough.

Light, healthy, and delicious, seafood is perfect for any occasion. Whether your passion is for scallops or squid, clams or crayfish, this international recipe collection is guaranteed to inspire you.

snacks & appetizers

This traditional tapas dish is perfect served with a cold beer. It is a simple recipe and can be whipped up in no time at all. This method of deep-frying will make the batter crisp, while the shrimp remain tender and juicy inside. Cook them in small batches so as not to reduce the temperature of the oil.

shrimp in overcoats

10 oz. uncooked shrimp, shell on

¾ cup all-purpose flour

1 teaspoon baking powder

a pinch of salt

a pinch of oak-smoked sweet Spanish paprika (*pimentón dulce*)

1 cup beer

oil, for deep-frying

lemon wedges, for serving

an electric deep-fryer

SERVES 4

Peel the shrimp, but leave the tail fins intact. Sift the flour, baking powder, salt, and paprika into a bowl, mix well, then gently stir in the beer. Let rest for a few minutes.

Fill a deep-fryer with oil to the manufacturer's recommended level and heat the oil to 380°F. Dip the shrimp in the batter, then fry in the hot oil, in small batches, until golden brown. Remove from the oil, drain on paper towels, and keep them warm while you fry the remaining batches. Serve hot with lemon wedges.

spicy crab in phyllo cups

3 sheets phyllo pastry dough, each one about 14 x 18 inches

4 tablespoons butter, melted

Spicy crab filling

8 oz. canned crabmeat in brine, drained, about 1 cup

3 oz. (about ½ cup) canned water chestnuts, drained and finely chopped or sliced

1-inch piece of fresh ginger root, peeled and cut into thin strips

2 scallions, trimmed and thinly sliced

finely grated zest and juice of 1 unwaxed lime

1 garlic clove, crushed

½ fresh red serrano chile, seeded and finely chopped

2 teaspoons sesame oil

2 tablespoons chopped fresh cilantro

sea salt and freshly ground black pepper

3 mini-muffin pans, 12 cups each, brushed with melted butter

MAKES ABOUT 30

These delicate bites are as light as air, but packed with fresh Asian flavors. Use canned crabmeat from the Pacific for these— not only does it taste very good, but there is no shell or messy bits to deal with if you're catering for a large number of people. It is also much cheaper than fresh crab.

Unroll the phyllo and cut the stack into 90 pieces, roughly 3 inches square. To do this, keep the sheets stacked on top of each other, then mark the top sheet into 30 rough squares. Cut down through all 3 sheets, giving 90 squares. Pile the squares into 2 to 3 stacks, place in a plastic bag, and keep beside you.

To make a phyllo cup, take 3 squares of phyllo, brush each with melted butter, and set one on top of the other, so that the points make a star, and do not touch each other. Quickly but gently press into one of the cups of the prepared muffin pan, so the points of the phyllo shoot upwards like a handkerchief. Repeat with all the remaining phyllo until you have 30 cups.

Bake in a preheated oven at 350°F for 8 to 10 minutes until golden. Remove from the oven, let cool in the pan, then carefully remove to a tray (they are very fragile).

Put the crab in a bowl and fluff up with a fork. Stir in the water chestnuts, ginger, and scallions. In a separate bowl, mix the lime zest and juice, crushed garlic, chile, and sesame oil, and season to taste with salt and pepper. Mix this into the crab mixture (this can be done up to 4 hours in advance), then stir in the cilantro.

Fill the cups with the crab mixture just before serving (they can go a little soggy if they are kept too long).

The contrast of the golden crunchy bread crumbs and the soft mussel meat is fantastic. Cooking mussels in this way is typically Italian and really delicious. Although this recipe may seem a lot of work, it is well worth it.

baked mussels
with crispy bread crumbs

3 lb. fresh mussels, in the shell

⅔ cup white wine

2 garlic cloves, lightly crushed

3 tablespoons olive oil, plus extra for sprinkling

1 onion, very finely chopped

1 cup stale but not dried bread crumbs

¼ cup finely chopped fresh flat-leaf parsley

freshly squeezed juice of 1 lemon

sea salt and freshly ground black pepper

a large baking dish or 4 individual baking dishes

a baking sheet

SERVES 4

Scrub and debeard the mussels. Tap them all against the counter and discard any that don't close—they are dead—and also any with damaged shells.

Put the mussels in a large saucepan, add the wine and garlic, cover tightly with a lid, and cook over high heat for 4 to 5 minutes until they just start to open. Discard any that do not open. Strain through a colander and reserve the juices.

When the mussels have cooled, twist off all the empty half-shells and arrange the mussels in a single layer in a large baking dish or individual baking dishes set on a baking sheet.

Heat the olive oil in a skillet, add the onion, and sauté for about 5 minutes until soft. Reduce the heat, add the parsley and bread crumbs, and stir well so all the bread crumbs absorb the oil. Cook for another 5 minutes to brown the bread crumbs a little.

Sprinkle this mixture over the mussels, trickle some extra olive oil and the lemon juice over them, and bake in a preheated oven at 425°F for 5 minutes. Reheat the strained mussel liquid in a saucepan, add salt and pepper to taste (take care because it may already be salty), then pour it around the mussels before serving, if you like.

spanish clams
with ham

1 lb. small fresh clams, such as littlenecks, in the shell

2 tablespoons extra virgin olive oil

2 oz. *jamón serrano* or prosciutto, cut into thin strips

1 small fresh green chile, seeded and chopped

2 garlic cloves, sliced

¼ cup white wine

2 tablespoons chopped scallion tops, chives, or parsley

SERVES 4

Mediterranean live clams usually go straight into the cooking pot, with oil and garlic. Herbs and a splash of wine are sometimes added. However, because Spanish cured hams are so exceptional, adding even a little seasons and enlivens many such savory dishes. Mar i montaña *(sea and mountain) is a typically Catalan cooking idea which has spread worldwide.*

Tap all the clams against the counter and discard any that don't close—they are dead—and any with damaged shells.

Put the olive oil, clams, ham, chile, and garlic in a large, heavy saucepan and stir over high heat. When the ham is cooked and the clams begin to open, add the wine, cover the pan, and tilt it several times to mix the ingredients. Cook over high heat for another 2 to 3 minutes or until all the clams have opened and are cooked (discard any that do not open).

Sprinkle with chopped scallions, chives, or parsley. Cover and cook for 1 minute more, then ladle into shallow soup bowls and serve immediately.

sizzled scallops with lemon

Scallops are a popular seafood in Italy. Allow three or four scallops per person, depending on their size, your appetite, and your budget. If using frozen scallops, they must be fully thawed, patted dry, and cooked more carefully, because they absorb a lot of water and create more steam.

Put 1 teaspoon of the lemon zest in a bowl, add the sea salt and garlic, and mix gently.

Pat the scallops dry with paper towels and add to the bowl.

Heat a nonstick skillet, add the butter and olive oil, and heat until sizzling. Add the scallops and cook for 1 to 1½ minutes on each side or until golden. The inside should be barely heated through, barely cooked, silky smooth, and opaque.

Reduce the heat and add the lemon juice and wine or vermouth to the skillet. Push the scallops to one side and tilt the pan to pool the juices. Add the mascarpone or cream cheese, if using, and stir it into the sauce. Heat until the sauce thickens slightly and evaporates to a creamy glaze.

Serve the scallops inside the deep shells or on small plates with the sauce spooned over them. Sprinkle with some freshly ground black pepper and accompany by slices of lemon and toasted ciabatta.

finely grated zest and freshly squeezed juice of 1 unwaxed lemon

1 teaspoon sea salt

2 garlic cloves, crushed

12–16 prepared scallops, and their deep shells if available

4 tablespoons butter

2 tablespoons extra virgin olive oil

2 tablespoons white wine or vermouth

2 tablespoons mascarpone or cream cheese, cut into small pieces (optional)

freshly ground black pepper

For serving

1 lemon, cut in half and sliced

sliced ciabatta bread, toasted

SERVES 4–6

squid with mayonnaise

Cuttlefish or squid, either whole tiny ones or larger ones sliced into rings, are favorites all around the Mediterranean, and in good bars and restaurants worldwide. In Spain, they are dipped in flour and sizzled in hot oil until crisp, often accompanied by a stinging, garlicky mayonnaise called alioli.

about 1 cup semolina flour

1 teaspoon sea salt

1 teaspoon dried oregano or marjoram leaves, crumbled

8 medium squid tubes, sliced into ½-inch rings

2 cups virgin olive oil, for deep-frying

2 lemons, cut in half, for serving

Alioli

6–8 fat garlic cloves, crushed

½ teaspoon sea salt

½ cup extra virgin olive oil

an electric deep-fryer

SERVES 4

Put the semolina flour, salt, and oregano or marjoram in a bowl. Pat the squid rings dry with paper towels and toss them in the flour mixture until well coated. Set them aside, not touching each other, while you make the sauce.

To make the alioli, put the garlic and salt in a mortar and crush to a sticky paste with a pestle. Pour in the oil in a fine stream, beating constantly in one direction until creamy. Continue adding the oil and mixing to form a thick, glossy emulsion. Alternatively, use a bowl and a hand-held beater.

Fill a deep-fryer with oil to the manufacturer's recommended level and heat to 375°F. Fry the prepared squid or cuttlefish in the hot oil in batches of about 8. Cook for 30 to 45 seconds, the minimum time it takes to set the seafood to firm whiteness and make the coating crisp. Remove from the oil, drain on paper towels, and keep hot. Continue frying the squid in batches until all are cooked.

Serve a pile of squid rings on each of 4 plates with ½ lemon for squeezing and a large spoonful of the alioli beside it or in bowls.

Variation Provençal aïoli, another version of alioli, can be made in a food processor, but the quantities must be larger to let the blades run. Put the garlic and salt from the main recipe in a food processor, add 2 egg yolks and 1 whole egg, and blend until creamy. Gradually pour in about ¾ cup olive oil until the mixture is thick and emulsified. You will find it becomes very thick. Blend in 1 to 2 tablespoons freshly squeezed lemon juice at the end. This quantity will serve 8 (more than the main recipe). If making ahead of time, cover closely with plastic wrap and keep in the refrigerator for up to 3 days.

Calamaretti (baby squid) are a favorite in Italy, especially in seaside trattorias. If your supermarket's fish counter doesn't have fresh baby squid, they will almost certainly have fresh or frozen prepared squid bodies. Buy the smallest you can find, fill them loosely with the stuffing, and cook for a few minutes more until firm and densely white. You will miss out on the crisp tentacles and the flavorful pink skins, but the dish will still taste good.

stuffed oven-roasted baby squid

1 lb. whole baby squid, fresh or frozen and thawed

½ teaspoon sea salt

¼ teaspoon hot red pepper flakes or crushed black peppercorns

¼ –⅓ cup extra virgin olive oil

Herb stuffing

2 tablespoons chopped fresh marjoram, oregano, or dill

¼ cup chopped fresh flat-leaf parsley

2 slices prosciutto or cooked ham, chopped

2 teaspoons grated unwaxed lemon zest

2 slices of stale white bread, crumbled

wooden toothpicks

SERVES 4–6

To make the stuffing, put the herbs, prosciutto or ham, lemon zest, and bread in a food processor and chop in a series of brief pulses. The mixture should be coarse.

To prepare the squid, wash it, then drain and pat dry with paper towels. Pull the tentacles out of the bodies. Trim off and discard the eyes and tiny beak in the middle of the star of tentacles. Rinse out the contents of the body and discard the transparent quill. Some people remove the pinky mauve skin, but you can leave it as it adds flavor and color.

Loosely pack the stuffing mixture inside the squid bodies and close the ends with a toothpick. Dust the stuffed squid and the tentacles with the salt and hot red pepper flakes or pepper. Arrange them in a shallow roasting pan.

Put the olive oil in a saucepan and heat until hot. Pour it over the squid and roast toward the top of a preheated oven at 400°F for 5 to 8 minutes or until the flesh sets white and firm and the stuffing smells aromatic. Serve hot or warm.

marinated octopus

Some people avoid cooking octopus because they think it can be tough. In Spain, fresh octopus are banged against the jetty by the fishermen to make them tender. If you don't have a fisherman on hand, buy octopus frozen (freezing also helps tenderize them). Then you should cook them long and slow at a low temperature. Octopus keeps well, and the longer you marinate it, the better the flavor.

Bring a large saucepan of water to a boil, then add the octopus and blanch for 30 seconds at a time, repeating 4 to 5 times. Return the octopus to the saucepan, cover with a lid, and simmer for 1 hour.

Test the octopus for tenderness—if it's still tough, continue cooking for another 20 minutes. Remove from the heat, let cool, then drain. Cut the tentacles into 1-inch lengths.

Heat the oil in a skillet, add the vinegar, garlic, 2 tablespoons of the parsley, the paprika, pepper flakes, capers, and octopus. Bring to a boil, then simmer for 3 minutes. Transfer to a plastic or ceramic dish, let cool, season with salt and pepper, then let marinate in the refrigerator overnight.

Serve at room temperature with the lemon juice and the remaining parsley sprinkled over the top.

about 12 oz. small octopus tentacles

3 tablespoons fruity olive oil

2 tablespoons red wine vinegar

2 garlic cloves, crushed

3 tablespoons chopped fresh flat-leaf parsley

½ teaspoon oak-smoked sweet Spanish paprika (*pimentón dulce*)

½ teaspoon hot red pepper flakes

1 tablespoon capers, chopped

freshly squeezed juice of 1 lemon

sea salt and freshly ground black pepper

SERVES 4

salads

This method of cooking mussels, based on the traditional recipe of mussels in white wine and garlic, makes a perfect summer salad.

mussels in ice wine

4 lb. large fresh mussels,
in the shell

1 cup fruity white wine, such
as Chardonnay

3 garlic cloves, crushed

1 small onion, chopped

a sprig of fresh thyme

1 bay leaf

2 sprigs of fresh parsley

a handful of chives, chopped

ice cubes, to serve

SERVES 4–6

Scrub and debeard the mussels. Tap them all against the counter and discard any that don't close—they are dead—and any with damaged shells.

Put a layer of ice cubes in a small roasting dish and put a wire rack on top.

Put the wine, garlic, onion, thyme, bay leaf, and parsley in a large saucepan and bring to a boil. Working in batches, add the prepared mussels, put on the lid, and let steam until they open, 1 to 2 minutes. Remove the mussels from the pan with a straining spoon as they open. Discard any that don't open. Take the empty shell off the top and put the mussel in its bottom shell on the rack over ice. Repeat with the remaining batches of mussels.

When the mussels are cool, cover with plastic wrap and keep in the refrigerator until ready to serve. Check from time to time that the melted ice isn't flooding them—pour it off if it does, so the water doesn't dilute the mussel flavor.

Strain the cooking liquid. It may be gritty, so strain through cheesecloth if necessary. Let cool, then chill in the refrigerator.

Put a serving platter in the freezer. When ready to serve, spread a layer of ice cubes on the platter and arrange the mussels on top. Sprinkle with chopped chives, then spoon the cooking liquid over the top—you need a little in each shell.

spicy thai shrimp salad

1 tablespoon peanut oil

1 tablespoon Thai red
curry paste

12 uncooked shrimp, shelled,
deveined, and cut in
half lengthwise

12 cherry tomatoes, cut in half

a handful of fresh mint sprigs,
for serving

Spicy Thai dressing

1 stalk of lemongrass, outer
leaves discarded, remainder
very finely chopped

2 fresh red Thai chiles, thinly
sliced and seeded, if preferred

2 Thai pink shallots or
1 small regular shallot,
thinly sliced lengthwise

1 tablespoon brown sugar
or palm sugar

freshly squeezed juice of
2 unwaxed limes

grated zest of 2 kaffir limes

a handful of fresh cilantro,
finely chopped

3 scallions, finely chopped

2 kaffir lime leaves, mid-rib
removed, the leaves very
thinly sliced crosswise,
then finely chopped

SERVES 4

This salad is very simple—you can also make it with precooked shrimp. Cutting the shrimp in half lengthwise makes them easier to eat and also makes them curl into pretty corkscrews when they are stir-fried. When preparing the lemongrass and kaffir lime leaves, make sure to slice them very thinly indeed. If you can't find them, use a squeeze of lemon juice instead of the lemongrass and some grated regular lime zest instead of the kaffir lime leaves. The grated zest of kaffir limes is much more scented and delicious than that of regular limes, which can be used if you can't find the real thing. Kaffir is a Hindi word meaning "foreign," so throughout history people have thought these limes looked a little unusual.

Heat the oil and curry paste in a wok, add the shrimp, and stir-fry for about 1 minute until opaque. Let cool.

To make the dressing, crush the lemongrass, 1 chile, and half the shallots with a mortar and pestle. Add the sugar, lime juice, and zest, and mix well until the sugar dissolves. Stir in the remaining chile and shallots, the cilantro, scallions, and lime leaves.

Put the shrimp in a serving bowl, add the cherry tomatoes, pour the dressing over the top, and toss well. Serve, topped with mint sprigs.

Variations

• This dressing is also good with crab claws, either stir-fried or boiled.

• Use scallops instead of shrimp.

• Try other Thai curry pastes, or a mixture of peanut oil and toasted sesame oil.

August is crayfish season in Sweden, when the stores are full of special crayfish party paraphernalia—paper hats, paper lanterns with sunny faces, and candles for the table. Crayfish are traditional, but the dish is equally good made with large shrimp.

swedish crayfish party

2 tablespoons sea salt

3 tablespoons dill seed

a large bunch of fresh dill, tied up with kitchen twine

10–20 uncooked crayfish or shrimp per person

For serving

a small bunch of fresh dill, preferably with flower heads

toast or crusty bread

unsalted butter

iced aquavit or vodka

beer

mayonnaise (optional)

SERVES 4–6

To cook the crayfish, start the day before. Put the salt, dill seed, and bundle of dill in a large saucepan, add 2½ quarts water, and bring to a rolling boil. Add the crayfish, 5 to 6 at a time, to the boiling water. Cover with a lid and simmer for about 5 minutes, or just until they turn red. Like all seafood, they shouldn't be cooked too long or they will be tough.

Remove the crayfish with a slotted spoon and transfer to a large bowl. Tuck more fresh dill between them. When all the crayfish are cooked, put the saucepan in a bowl of cold water to bring down the temperature quickly. When a little cooler, strain the liquid over the crayfish and let cool completely. Keep in the refrigerator overnight or for up to 24 hours.

If using ready-cooked crayfish or shrimp, put them in a bowl with some fresh dill. Boil the water with the salt, dill seeds, and bunch of dill, let cool, then strain over the crayfish and chill as before.

When ready to serve, drain the crayfish and pile generously onto a large serving platter. Top with the small bunch of dill and serve with toast or bread, lots of good butter for spreading, aquavit or vodka, and beer. Provide lobster crackers and picks, big table napkins, and finger bowls.

To eat the crayfish, remove its claws and crack them. Eat the meat with your fingers. Pull off the tail and cut it down the side. Pull out the tail meat and remove and discard the dark thread. Eat on buttered toast or bread—or all alone. You could serve the crayfish with a bowl of mayonnaise for dipping, if you like, but it's not traditional.

greek octopus salad

Greeks are in love with octopus and squid. This deliciously fresh salad is guaranteed to transport you to the sunny islands of Greece. If you have a Greek fish vendor, he will remove the beak, eyes, and insides of the octopus for you. If not, it is very easy to do this yourself (see note, below).

Put the octopus in a large saucepan, cover with water, and bring to a boil. Add the potato, garlic, oregano, and dill, and return to a boil. Reduce the heat and simmer until the potato is cooked. When it is cooked, so is the octopus: it will take about 30 minutes.

Remove the octopus from the pot. Rub off the skin (if preferred) and remove the suckers. Cut the octopus into bite-size pieces.

Put the dressing ingredients in a large bowl and beat with a fork. Add the octopus and toss to coat. Chill until you are ready to serve. Serve the octopus topped with sprigs of basil and dill and some chopped parsley.

*Notes

• To clean a large octopus, turn it upside down so the tentacles form a star. In the middle of the star is the hard beak. Cut it out and discard it. Make a slit down the body and rinse it out. Remove and discard the transparent quill.

• If you don't want to cook the octopus whole, prepare it like a squid. Pull off the tentacles—the insides should come out, too. Cut the tentacles off just above their join, so they make a star. Cut out the beak as before. Rinse out the body. Keep the tentacles and body and discard the rest.

1–2 octopus, (2–4 lb. total), cleaned*

1 large potato, peeled but left whole

3 garlic cloves, crushed

a sprig of fresh oregano

2–3 sprigs of fresh dill

Green herb dressing

5–6 tablespoons extra virgin olive oil

freshly squeezed juice of ½–1 lemon

a handful of fresh basil leaves, thinly sliced

leaves from a sprig of fresh oregano, chopped

1 tablespoon chopped fresh dill

sea salt and freshly ground black pepper

For serving

sprigs of fresh basil

sprigs of fresh dill

2 tablespoons chopped fresh parsley

SERVES 8–10

char-grilled scallop salad

It is important not to overcook scallops: cook them only until they become opaque (the time depends on their size). When you buy them, ask for dry scallops. Often, they've been soaked in a special solution—they sponge up about 30 percent of their own weight given half a chance. As soon as they hit the pan, they drop it all and look limp and flaccid: you've paid good money for water! Serve this warm salad with a dry white wine.

8 oz. shelled green peas (fresh or frozen) or shelled fava beans, about 1½ cups

salad greens

8 very thin slices of pancetta or bacon

about 20 shelled scallops

¼ cup extra virgin olive oil

4 teaspoons white rice vinegar

sea salt and freshly ground black pepper

SERVES 4

Microwave the peas or fava beans on HIGH for 2 minutes. Cool under cold running water, then transfer to a bowl of ice cubes and water. If using fava beans, as soon as they are cool enough to handle, pop them out of their gray skins. Discard the skins and reserve the beans. Alternatively, boil or steam the peas or beans until tender. If using frozen peas, follow the package instructions.

Arrange the salad greens on 4 plates.

Heat a stovetop grill pan or nonstick skillet, add the pancetta or bacon, and cook until crisp and brown on both sides. Drain on paper towels. Add the scallops to the pan and cook over high heat for 1 to 2 minutes on each side until browned on the outside and opaque all the way through. Do not overcook or the scallops will shrink and be tough.

Drain the peas or beans and divide them and the bacon between the plates. As soon as the scallops are cooked, add about 5 to each plate. Serve immediately, sprinkled with olive oil, vinegar, salt, and pepper.

soups

Although Westerners like to have soup as a separate course, in Thailand it is served with other dishes. People ladle spoonfuls of soup from a communal bowl onto the rice on their plates. This soup, known as Tom Yam Kung, *is a traditional Thai recipe, with an aroma created by kaffir lime leaves and lemongrass. It is a must on the menu in all Thai restaurants, and easy to make at home.*

hot and sour soup
with shrimp

5 cups chicken broth

1 tablespoon tom yam sauce*

2 stalks of tender lemongrass, coarsely sliced

4 kaffir lime leaves, finely chopped

3 tablespoons freshly squeezed lemon or lime juice

3 tablespoons Thai fish sauce

2 small fresh red or green chiles, thinly sliced

2 teaspoons sugar

12 straw mushrooms, cut in half (canned mushrooms will do)

12 uncooked jumbo shrimp, shelled, but with tail fins intact, and deveined

Heat the broth in a saucepan and add the tom yam sauce. Stir in the lemongrass, lime leaves, lemon or lime juice, fish sauce, chiles, and sugar. Bring to a boil and simmer for 2 minutes. Add the mushrooms and shrimp, stir, and cook for 2 to 3 minutes more, or until the shrimp are cooked through. Ladle into soup bowls and serve.

*Note Tom yam sauce is widely available, even in some supermarkets. If you can't find it, try an Asian grocery store.

SERVES 4

laksa lemak

1 lb. uncooked shrimp, shelled

2 tablespoons peanut oil

6 cups chicken stock

1 stalk of lemongrass, cut in half

2 kaffir lime leaves

2 sprigs of fresh lemon balm

4 thin slices of fresh ginger root

1 teaspoon light soy sauce

1¾ cups canned coconut milk

4 oz. bean sprouts, rinsed and trimmed, 1½–2 cups

brown sugar, to taste

a bunch of cilantro, chopped

sea salt

Laksa spice paste

a tiny piece of shrimp paste

4 small fresh red chiles, seeded

1 stalk of lemongrass

6 shallots, coarsely chopped

1 teaspoon ground turmeric

1 garlic clove, chopped

½ teaspoon ground ginger

6 macadamia nuts

2 tablespoons Thai fish sauce

For serving

8 oz. thick Chinese egg noodles, freshly cooked and drained

4 inches cucumber, thinly sliced

a handful of Napa cabbage

SERVES 4–6

Laksa, the spicy shrimp and noodle soup from Malaysia and Singapore, has become fashionable all over the world. This one is a specialty of the Nonya or Straits-Chinese community. Its bright yellow color comes from turmeric and, on its home ground, fresh turmeric is often used rather than the ground turmeric found in the West.

To make the laksa spice paste, toast the shrimp paste in a small dry skillet, then transfer to a blender. Finely chop the chiles. Discard the outer leaves of the lemongrass and chop the remainder very finely. Add the chiles and lemongrass to the blender, along with all the other spice paste ingredients. Grind to a thick, chunky paste. You may need to add a little water to let the blades run. Alternatively, grind all the ingredients with a mortar and pestle.

Remove the black veins from the shrimp and set aside.

Heat the oil in a large saucepan and add the laksa paste. Sauté for about 8 minutes. Add the chicken broth, lemongrass, lime leaves, lemon balm, ginger, and soy sauce. Bring to a boil and add the coconut milk, stirring to keep it from separating. Reduce the heat and simmer gently for 15 minutes.

Add the shrimp, bean sprouts, sugar, and salt and simmer for 2 to 3 minutes until the shrimp are just cooked. Discard the lemon balm and lemongrass and add the chopped cilantro.

To serve, shred the Napa cabbage and put it, along with the noodles and cucumber, in 4 large or 6 smaller bowls, then ladle the soup over the top.

Note If you have the time, leave the broth, minus the shrimp, for 1 hour or more for the flavors to mingle and mellow. Add the shrimp just before you are ready to serve. Do not use ready-cooked shrimp: their tough texture will spoil the dish.

thai lobster noodle soup

Like so much Thai food, this recipe has a delicate balance of spicy, fresh, zesty flavors. Kaffir lime leaves are increasingly available, either as part of a Thai flavor package in supermarkets, or in bags from Asian or Chinatown markets. Buy the whole bag and freeze them, then use straight from frozen. Ginger can also be frozen, then grated from frozen. Both flavors contrast well with the richness of coconut milk and lobster. Seaweed and sesame seeds aren't traditional—less Thai than Japanese, but no less delicious for all that.

Put the lobster or crayfish shells, dried shrimp, and kaffir lime leaves in a large saucepan. Add 6 cups water and bring to a boil, then reduce the heat and simmer for 1 hour. Strain the broth. Grate the ginger, and squeeze the juice from it into the broth.

Soak the noodles in a bowl of cold water for 20 minutes. When soft, drain well and cover until needed. Put the seaweed in a bowl and stir in the mirin.

Add the coconut cream to the broth, stir well, and bring to a boil. Reduce the heat, then add fish sauce and lime juice to taste.

When ready to serve, add the drained noodles to the broth and reheat. Ladle into hot bowls, then add the chiles, chives, beans, and lobster or crayfish meat. Drain the seaweed and sprinkle it over the soup, then top with Thai sweet basil leaves, and serve.

Note Fish vendors and Chinese supermarkets often have frozen crayfish tails, which are good for this recipe. Instead of hijiki seaweed, you could sprinkle some black sesame seeds on top.

2 small cooked lobsters or crayfish tails, shells removed and reserved

4 oz. dried shrimp, about 1 cup

3 kaffir lime leaves, torn

1-inch piece of fresh ginger root, peeled

8 oz. dried wide rice noodles (*sen lek*)

2 tablespoons hijiki seaweed

2 tablespoons mirin (sweetened Japanese rice wine)

¾ cup coconut cream

about 2 tablespoons Thai fish sauce

freshly squeezed juice of 1 lime

2 fresh mild red chiles, cut in half lengthwise, seeded, and thinly sliced

2 fresh mild green chiles, cut in half lengthwise, seeded, and thinly sliced

a handful of garlic chives, sliced diagonally, or use regular chives and 1 crushed garlic clove

½ cup thin green beans, sliced in half lengthwise and cooked

2 sprigs of fresh Thai sweet basil leaves (optional)

SERVES 4

There are many kinds of chowder—this New England variety, made with clams and cream; the Manhattan kind, made with clams and tomatoes; and the British kind, made with corn and smoked haddock instead of the clams.

clam chowder

4 lb. fresh quahog clams, in the shell

½ cup fish stock or clam juice, plus extra fish stock to make 1 quart

1 lb. smoked pancetta or prosciutto, cut into cubes

safflower oil (optional)

3 onions, coarsely chopped

1 celery stalk, chopped

1 carrot, chopped

2 bay leaves

a few sprigs of fresh thyme

8 oz. boiling potatoes, peeled and cut into cubes, 1½–1¾ cups

2 cups heavy cream

sea salt and freshly cracked black pepper

For serving

a large bunch of flat-leaf parsley, coarsely chopped

oyster crackers

SERVES 4

Put the clams in a large saucepan, then add ½ cup water and the fish stock or clam juice. Cover the pan, bring to a boil, and boil hard for a few minutes until the clams open. Remove them as soon as they do and shuck them over a bowl. Don't overcook them or they will be tough. Discard the shells, reserve the clams, and return the juice in the bowl to the pan. (Discard any clams that have not opened.) Strain the cooking liquid through a strainer, then through cheesecloth into a large glass measuring cup. Add enough fish stock to make up to 1 quart. Reserve.

Clean the pan, add the pancetta, and cook over low heat to render the fat (add a dash of safflower oil to encourage it if you like). Remove the crisp pancetta and set aside.

Add the onions, celery, carrot, bay leaves, and thyme to the fat in the pan. Cook gently until the onions are softened and translucent. Add the cubes of potato and the reserved 1 quart stock, and simmer until the potatoes are done, about 10 minutes.

Chop half the clams, and cut the others in half through their thickness. Add the clams, pancetta, and cream to the saucepan and heat through. Taste and add salt if necessary (remember the clam juices and pancetta are already salty). Remove and discard the bay leaves and thyme.

Ladle into warm soup bowls and serve sprinkled with lots of cracked pepper, crisp pancetta, and handfuls of parsley, and with oyster crackers on the side.

bouillabaisse

1½ lb. fresh mussels, in the shell

¼ cup extra virgin olive oil

4 garlic cloves, crushed

2 cups dry white wine

a small bunch of flat-leaf parsley

a pinch of cayenne

a small bunch of thyme

5 cups water or fish stock

a large pinch of saffron strands

1 head fennel, sliced lengthwise

4 large ripe tomatoes, cubed

4 lb. assorted prepared white fish: such as cod, snapper, or monkfish (angler fish), cut into 2-inch chunks

¾ lb. prepared baby squid (see page 21), sliced or whole

2 tablespoons Pernod or Ricard, to taste (optional)

sea salt flakes

Croûtes

olive oil, for sautéing

12–16 slices of French bread

4 garlic cloves, squashed, not peeled

½ cup rouille*

½ cup grated Gruyère cheese

SERVES 6–8

Scrub and debeard the mussels. Tap them all against the counter and discard any that don't close—they are dead—and any with damaged shells.

Heat 2 tablespoons olive oil in a very large, high-sided saucepan. Add the mussels, garlic, and wine. Cover the pan and shake over medium heat for 4 to 6 minutes or until all the mussels have opened (discard any that remain closed).

Remove the pan from the heat and tip into a colander lined with wet cheesecloth or paper towels set over a bowl to catch the juices. Remove and discard the shells from half the mussels. Set all the mussels aside and return the strained liquid to the pan. Tie the parsley and thyme into a bundle with twine, then add to the pan, together with the cayenne and water or stock.

Put a pinch of the saffron in the pan and crush the rest with 2 teaspoons sea salt using a mortar and pestle. Add a splash of liquid to dissolve the powder, then add it to the pan.

Add the fennel, tomatoes, and the fish to the pan and return to a boil. Reduce the heat and simmer, partially covered, for 6 to 8 minutes or until the fish is fairly well cooked. Add the squid and reserved mussels and cover the pan again just long enough to reheat the mussels and cook the squid until firm but not rubbery—about 1 minute. Uncover the pan, sprinkle with Pernod, if using, and set aside while you make the croûtes.

Heat a little olive oil in a skillet. Add the bread and sauté on both sides until golden. Rub the slices with the garlic and top them with the rouille and cheese.

To serve, put the croûtes in deep, heated soup plates, add a share of the fish, seafood, and liquid, and enjoy while the flavors, colors, and aromas are at their best.

*Note Rouille, a fiery rust-colored sauce, is available in cans or jars from large supermarkets.

entrées

In this quick, pan-fried curry, the flavor comes mainly from chile oil. As soon as the pan and oil are heated, add the clams, steam for just a few minutes, and they're cooked.

baby clams
with chile oil and holy basil

1 tablespoon peanut or
safflower oil

2 garlic cloves, finely chopped

2 lb. fresh baby clams,
in the shell

2 tablespoons Thai fish sauce

2 small fresh red chiles,
thinly sliced

20 holy basil leaves

Chile oil

2 tablespoons peanut or
safflower oil

¼ cup finely chopped garlic

¼ cup finely chopped shallots

¼ cup finely chopped
dried red chiles

½ teaspoon sea salt

1 tablespoon sugar

SERVES 4

To make the chile oil, heat the oil in a wok, add the garlic, and stir-fry until golden brown. Remove the garlic with a fine mesh scoop and set aside. Add the shallots to the wok and stir-fry until brown and crisp, then remove and set aside. Add the chiles to the wok and stir-fry until they begin to darken, then remove and set aside.

Using a mortar and pestle, pound the sautéed chiles, garlic, and shallots together. Return them to the wok and stir over low heat. Stir in the salt and sugar and mix to make a thick, slightly oily reddish-black sauce, not a paste. You will need 1 tablespoon for this recipe, reserve the rest for another use.

To cook the clams, heat the oil in a large skillet, add the garlic, and sauté until golden brown. Add 1 tablespoon chile oil and the baby clams and stir thoroughly. Add the fish sauce, chiles, and ¼ cup water. Stir thoroughly, add the basil, cover the pan, and let steam for a few minutes until the clams have opened. Discard any that don't open. Stir again, transfer to warmed dishes, and serve.

herb omelet with shrimp

Iran (Persia) boasts one of the world's great cuisines, and this herb omelet (coucou sabzi) is one of its best-known dishes. Shrimp have been added to make it a more substantial lunch dish. If you don't have a suitable oven dish, use a skillet with an ovenproof handle to finish off the cooking. Fennel leaves can be hard to find in stores because they wilt easily. If you can't find them, use the green sprouting tops from bulb fennel instead.

To prepare the shrimp, devein them by removing the black vein that runs down the back. "Butterfly" the shrimp by cutting down the back lengthwise, but leave the tail fins intact so they will sit upright when cooked.

Put the eggs in a bowl, add salt and pepper to taste and 2 tablespoons olive oil. Beat briefly with a fork or whisk.

Put 2 tablespoons olive oil in a skillet, heat gently, then add the chopped fennel and wilt for about 3 minutes. Add the scallions and leek, and stir to wilt a little. Stir into the egg mixture.

Put the leaves from the parsley, mint, oregano, and half the fennel fronds on a board. Chop them all together, then stir into the eggs. Pour into the prepared ovenproof dish, then sit the shrimp upright in the dish.

Cover carefully with foil and cook in a preheated oven at 350°F for 25 minutes, then uncover and continue baking until cooked and golden, about 5 minutes more. Tear half the remaining fennel fronds over the top. Set aside for a few minutes before serving.

Cut into wedges, to include at least 1 shrimp in each serving. Sprinkle with the remaining fennel fronds and serve with crusty bread and crisp salad greens.

6–8 uncooked shrimp, shelled, but with tail fins intact

6 extra-large eggs

5 tablespoons olive oil

½ cup milk

1 small bulb of fennel, thinly sliced, then chopped, and a large handful of the green leaves

3 scallions, thinly sliced

1 young leek, thinly sliced

4 sprigs of fresh parsley

4 sprigs of fresh mint

a small handful of fresh oregano leaves

a large handful of fennel fronds

sea salt and freshly ground black pepper

For serving

crusty bread

crisp salad greens

an ovenproof dish, 8 x 11 inches, preferably nonstick, oiled

SERVES 6

african seafood kabobs
with piri piri basting oil

The piri piri is a fiercely hot variety of chile introduced to Africa by the Portuguese, probably via Western India. The name is also used for the hot sauces in which the pods are used. Versions of piri piri sauce can be found in many former Portuguese colonies, from Mozambique and Angola to Brazil, as well as Portugal itself.

12 large, uncooked shrimp, shelled, but with tail fins intact

8–12 small sea scallops, muscles removed

12–20 fresh bay leaves

ciabatta or focaccia bread, for serving

Piri piri basting oil

3 garlic cloves, crushed

5–6 red Thai chiles or 8–9 red serrano chiles, seeded and coarsely chopped

freshly squeezed juice of ½ lemon

⅓–½ cup extra virgin olive oil

½ teaspoon nigella seeds (optional)

4 metal skewers

SERVES 4

To make the piri piri basting oil, put the garlic, chiles, lemon juice, and olive oil in a blender and process until smooth. Transfer to a bowl and stir in the nigella seeds, if using.

Dip the shrimp and scallops in the basting oil and coat well. Thread the shrimp and scallops alternately onto the skewers, with the bay leaves between them.

Lay the skewers on a broiler rack in a broiler tray, leaving room between them. Cook under a preheated hot broiler for about 5 minutes, basting frequently with the piri piri oil and turning once halfway through, until the shrimp and scallops are cooked. (Don't overcook or the scallops will be tough—shrimp and scallops are done when the flesh becomes opaque.) Alternatively, instead of basting the kabobs during broiling, put the piri piri oil in a small saucepan, boil for 1 to 2 minutes, then serve as a dipping sauce for the kabobs. Serve the kabobs with the bread.

2 tablespoons peanut or
safflower oil

2 garlic cloves, finely chopped

12 uncooked jumbo shrimp,
shelled and deveined

2¾ cups coconut cream

2¾ cups vegetable broth

2 large fresh red chiles, sliced
diagonally into thin ovals

¼ cup Thai fish sauce

8 round green Thai eggplants
(pea eggplants), quartered

1 tablespoon sugar

30 fresh Thai sweet basil leaves

Green curry paste

1 teaspoon coriander seeds

1 teaspoon cumin seeds

1 teaspoon white peppercorns

1 tablespoon chopped lemongrass

1-inch piece of fresh galangal or
ginger root, peeled and chopped

2 long green chiles, chopped

10 small green chiles, chopped

2 tablespoons chopped garlic

3 Thai pink shallots or
1 regular, chopped

3 cilantro roots, chopped

1 teaspoon finely chopped
kaffir lime leaves

2 teaspoons shrimp paste

SERVES 4

Green curry is a classic dish from Thailand. You can buy ready-made green curry paste from most supermarkets, but this homemade version is wonderful and well worth the effort.

green curry
with shrimp

To make the green curry paste, put all the paste ingredients in a large mortar and grind to a thick paste with a pestle.

Heat the oil in a large saucepan, add the garlic, and sauté until golden brown. Stir in 2 tablespoons of the green curry paste. Add the shrimp and stir-fry until just cooked through, about 1 minute. Add the coconut cream and bring to a boil, stirring constantly. Add the vegetable broth and return to a boil, stirring constantly.

Keeping the curry simmering, add the chiles, fish sauce, eggplants, and sugar and simmer until the eggplants are cooked but still crunchy (do not overcook or the shrimp will be tough).

Stir in the basil leaves just before pouring into serving bowls. Serve with rice and other Thai dishes.

Cheese pastry dough

2 cups all-purpose flour, plus extra for dusting

1 teaspoon salt

3 tablespoons freshly grated Parmesan cheese

9 tablespoons unsalted butter, chilled and cut into cubes

2 egg yolks

2–3 tablespoons ice water

Chile crab filling

2 tablespoons olive oil

a bunch of scallions, thinly sliced

6 eggs

1¼ cups heavy cream

1 tablespoon Dijon mustard

1 lb. fresh or frozen crabmeat, thawed and drained, about 2 cups

8 mild, sweet pickled red chile peppers, seeded and coarsely chopped

1 cup freshly grated Parmesan cheese

freshly ground black pepper

a deep removable-bottomed fluted tart pan, 10 inches diameter

foil or parchment paper and baking beans

a baking sheet

SERVES 6–8

crab and sweet pickled chile tart

The sweet and salty taste of fresh crab (if you can get it) mixed with mild red chiles pickled in sweet vinegar is fantastic. They seem made for each other. Serve this with an avocado salsa or just plain sliced avocado dressed with a cilantro vinaigrette.

To make the dough, sift the flour and salt into a bowl. Stir in the Parmesan, then rub in the butter with the tips of your fingers. Mix the egg yolks with 2 tablespoons ice water, then stir into the flour mixture to bind to a firm but malleable dough (if it is too dry, stir in another tablespoon of water). Knead lightly until smooth, then shape into a flattened ball. Wrap in plastic wrap and chill for at least 30 minutes.

Bring the dough to room temperature. Put the dough on a lightly floured counter, roll out to a thickness of ⅛ inch, and use to line the tart pan. Prick the pie shell all over with a fork, then chill or freeze for 15 minutes.

Line the pie shell with foil or parchment paper, then fill with baking beans. Set on a baking sheet and bake blind in the center of a preheated oven at 400°F for 10 to 12 minutes. Remove the foil or parchment paper and the baking beans, and return the pie crust to the oven for 5 to 7 minutes longer to dry out completely. Remove from the oven and let cool. Reduce the oven temperature to 350°F.

To make the filling, heat the olive oil in a saucepan, add the scallions, and sauté until softened but not colored. Let cool slightly. Put the eggs, cream, and mustard in a bowl and beat well. Stir in the crab, cooked scallions, sweet chile peppers, and Parmesan, then season with plenty of black pepper. Spoon into the pie crust and level the surface. Set on a baking sheet and bake for about 45 minutes until just firm.

Serve warm or at room temperature.

pasta & rice

seafood spaghettini

Vary the seafood depending on what's available and best on the day, but always include clams or mussels— for their flavor as well as their beautiful shells.

1 lb. fresh mussels or clams, in the shell

10 oz. dried pasta, such as spaghettini

¼ cup olive oil

10 oz. mixed seafood, such as squid, cut into rings, shelled shrimp, and scallops, cut in half crosswise

2 tablespoons chopped fresh flat-leaf parsley

sea salt and freshly ground black pepper

SERVES 4

Scrub and debeard the mussels, if using. Tap the mussels or clams against the counter and discard any that don't close— they are dead—and any with damaged shells.

Bring a large saucepan of water to a boil. Add a good pinch of salt, then the pasta, and cook until *al dente*, or according to the timings on the package.

Meanwhile, heat half the oil in a large sauté pan or saucepan. Add the mixed seafood and cook for 3 to 4 minutes, stirring constantly until just cooked. Transfer to a large bowl and set aside.

Add the mussels or clams to the seafood pan, cover with a lid, and cook for 5 minutes until all the shells have opened. Discard any that remain closed.

Drain the pasta well and return it to the warm pan. Add the mussels or clams, mixed seafood, parsley, and the remaining olive oil. Add salt and pepper to taste, toss gently to mix, then serve immediately.

A delicious, low fat pasta dish? Yes it's true.
Better still, it's ready to serve in 15 minutes.

mussels in white wine
with linguine

2¼ lb. fresh mussels,
in the shell

10 oz. dried pasta, such as
linguine or tagliatelle

⅔ cup dry white wine

2 garlic cloves, finely chopped

1 small fresh red chile, such as
serrano, seeded and
finely chopped

2 tablespoons chopped
fresh flat-leaf parsley

sea salt and freshly ground
black pepper

olive oil, for serving

SERVES 4

Scrub and debeard the mussels. Tap them all against the counter and discard any that don't close—they are dead—and any with damaged shells.

Bring a large saucepan of water to a boil. Add a good pinch of salt, then the pasta, and cook until *al dente*, or according to the timings on the package.

Meanwhile, put the wine, garlic, and chile in another large saucepan, bring to a boil, and simmer rapidly for 5 minutes. Season with freshly ground black pepper. Add the mussels, cover with a lid, and cook for 5 minutes, shaking the pan from time to time, until all the shells have opened. Discard any that remain closed.

Drain the pasta and return it to the warm pan. Add the parsley and mussels and toss gently. Divide between 4 bowls, sprinkle with olive oil, and serve immediately.

pappardelle
with seafood sauce

Homemade pasta is not as difficult as you might think, and pappardelle is easier to make than most. Olive oil is the perfect vehicle for sauces and marries well with elegant ingredients such as lobster, shrimp, or crab. It makes pasta a special-occasion dish.

To make the pappardelle, put the flour, eggs, and 2 teaspoons sea salt flakes in a food processor. Work in bursts for about 1 minute until the mixture comes together in a crumbly mass and then forms into a rough ball. Transfer to a floured counter, then knead it firmly by hand for 2 minutes. Wrap in plastic wrap and chill in the refrigerator for 1 hour.

Divide the dough into 4 parts, keeping 3 still wrapped. Starting on the thickest setting of the pasta machine, roll 1 piece of dough through, 3 to 4 times, folding the 2 ends into the middle each time to get a plump envelope of dough and giving it a half turn each time. Lightly flour the dough on both sides.

Roll it through all the settings on the pasta machine, starting at the thickest, about 6 times in all, until you get a 3-foot length of pasta (cut it in half if it's easier). Hang this over a chair or pole to air-dry. Repeat with the 3 remaining balls of dough. After air-drying, roll up each length of pasta, then slice into 1-inch-wide ribbons. Unroll, dust in semolina flour, then cut each in half, to make strips about 18 inches long.

To make the sauce, heat the oil in a heavy skillet. Add the lobster, shrimp, or crabmeat, dill, chives, 1 tablespoon lemon juice, salt, and pepper. Heat briefly until the flavors blend, then keep warm over very low heat.

Bring a large saucepan of water to a boil. Add a pinch of salt, then the pasta, and cook for 1½ minutes. Drain the pasta, then tip it into the sauce. Toss gently, add the lemon zest, and serve immediately in warmed bowls.

¾ cup extra virgin olive oil

1 lb. lobster meat, from 2 lb. whole lobster, or 2 cups shrimp or crabmeat

a bunch of dill, chopped, about 1 cup

a bunch of chives, chopped, about 1 cup

shredded zest and juice of 1 unwaxed lemon

sea salt and freshly crushed black pepper

Pappardelle

4 cups Italian tipo 00 flour*, plus extra for dusting

5 eggs

2 teaspoons sea salt flakes, crushed

semolina flour, for dusting

a pasta machine

SERVES 4

* Use this special Italian fine-grade flour (available from Italian specialty shops) to make your own pasta. If utterly unobtainable, use pasta flour or all-purpose flour instead. Alternatively, use dried pasta.

3 lb. assorted non-oily fish and shellfish, such as haddock, halibut, eel, crayfish, lobster, shrimp, crabs, mussels, and clams

1 teaspoon sea salt

4 garlic cloves, sliced

4 celery stalks, sliced

1 head of fennel, quartered

20 black peppercorns, crushed

12-inch strip of unwaxed orange zest

12-inch strip of unwaxed lemon zest

a large bunch of wild oregano or thyme, or 1 tablespoon dried herbs

1–2 tablespoons tomato paste

Cuscusu

2½ cups coarse "instant" couscous

1 onion, sliced

2 green chiles, thinly sliced

2 tablespoons extra virgin olive oil

3 cups boiling seafood stock or hot water

1 teaspoon orange flower water (optional)

freshly squeezed juice of 1 orange

sea salt and freshly ground black pepper

SERVES 4–6

seafood with couscous

In this delicious recipe, originally from Trapani in Sicily, a generous fish stew is ladled over the aromatic cuscusu *and the juices add their flavor to its fragrant charms. Modern "instant" or precooked couscous is quick and easy because it needs only moistening and heating—a bonus, because cooking traditional North African couscous requires skill and is very time-consuming.*

Cut the fish and shellfish into 1-inch chunks or, if small, leave them whole. Put in a very large, heavy saucepan, add the salt, garlic, celery, fennel, peppercorns, and 2 cups water, and bring to a boil. Stir in the orange and lemon zest, oregano, and enough tomato paste to make the liquid rosy. Reduce the heat to a simmer. Cover and cook for 10 minutes.

To prepare the *cuscusu*, put the couscous, onion, chiles, olive oil, salt, and pepper in a heatproof bowl. Pour in the boiling stock or water. Stir and leave for 5 minutes to plump up. Stir in the orange flower water. When all the liquid has been absorbed, add the orange juice.

Put the *cuscusu* in deep serving bowls and spoon the fish and its broth over the top and serve.

You can make this with fresh or frozen prepared squid. If you have the tentacles, they make a great topping—just quickly sear them on a stovetop grill pan. You could sauté a little extra sliced garlic and some chopped red chile in olive oil and pour this over the risotto before serving, if you like.

squid risotto

10 oz. squid, fresh or frozen and thawed

about 6 cups hot chicken or vegetable broth

1 stick unsalted butter

1 onion or 2 shallots, finely chopped

2–3 large garlic cloves, finely chopped

⅓ cup dry white wine

1½ cups risotto rice, preferably carnaroli

2 tablespoons chopped fresh parsley

1–2 tablespoons olive oil

sea salt and freshly ground black pepper

a stovetop grill pan or skillet (optional)

SERVES 4

To prepare the squid, see page 21. Cut the squid into rings or small pieces and reserve the tentacles, if using.

Put the broth in a saucepan and keep at a gentle simmer. Melt half the butter in a large, heavy saucepan and add the onion or shallots and the garlic. Cook gently for 5 minutes until translucent but not browned. Add the squid, then the wine, and cook gently for 5 minutes until the squid is white and the wine beginning to disappear. Add the rice and stir until well coated with the butter, wine, and squid, and heated through.

Begin adding the broth, a large ladle at a time, stirring gently until each ladle has almost been absorbed by the rice. The risotto should be kept at a bare simmer throughout cooking, so don't let the rice dry out—add more broth as necessary. Continue until the rice is tender and creamy, but the grains still firm. (This should take 15 to 20 minutes depending on the type of rice used—check the package instructions.)

Taste and season well with salt and pepper and beat in the remaining butter and the parsley. Cover and let rest for a couple of minutes.

Meanwhile, if using the tentacles, toss them in the olive oil to coat. Heat a stovetop grill pan to smoking hot and add the tentacles to the pan. Cook for 1 to 2 minutes, then remove to a plate.

Check the risotto—you may want to add a little more hot broth just before you serve to loosen it. Don't let it wait around too long or the rice will turn mushy. Serve with the tentacles on top.

index

recipe credits

Julz Beresford
Pages 9, 22

Vatcharin Bhumichitr
Pages 35, 45, 50

Maxine Clark
Pages 10, 13, 53, 62

Clare Ferguson
Pages 14, 17, 18, 21, 43,
58, 61

Silvana Franco
Pages 55, 57

Manisha Gambhir Harkins
Pages 36, 49

Elsa Petersen-Schepelern
Pages 25, 26, 29, 30,
33, 40

Linda Tubby
Pages 39, 46

photography credits

Martin Brigdale
Pages 2, 3, 7, 11, 12, 15, 19,
25, 52, 60, 63

Peter Cassidy
Pages 8–9, 16, 20, 23,
24–25, 27, 28, 31, 32,
34–35, 37, 38, 41, 42,
44–45, 45, 47, 48, 51,
55, 59

William Lingwood
Pages 1, 4–5, 36, 54–55,
56

David Montgomery
Page 9

Ian Wallace
Page 6

conversion chart

Weights and measures are rounded up
or down slightly to make measuring easier.

Volume equivalents

American	Metric	Imperial
1 teaspoon	5 ml	
1 tablespoon	15 ml	
¼ cup	60 ml	2 fl.oz.
⅓ cup	75 ml	2½ fl.oz.
½ cup	125 ml	4 fl.oz.
⅔ cup	150 ml	5 fl.oz. (¼ pint)
¾ cup	175 ml	6 fl.oz.
1 cup	250 ml	8 fl.oz.

Weight equivalents | | Measurements

Imperial	Metric	Inches	cm
1 oz.	25 g	¼ inch	5 mm
2 oz.	50 g	½ inch	1 cm
3 oz.	75 g	¾ inch	1.5 cm
4 oz.	125 g	1 inch	2.5 cm
5 oz.	150 g	2 inches	5 cm
6 oz.	175 g	3 inches	7 cm
7 oz.	200 g	4 inches	10 cm
8 oz. (½ lb.)	250 g	5 inches	12 cm
9 oz.	275 g	6 inches	15 cm
10 oz.	300 g	7 inches	18 cm
11 oz.	325 g	8 inches	20 cm
12 oz.	375 g	9 inches	23 cm
13 oz.	400 g	10 inches	25 cm
14 oz.	425 g	11 inches	28 cm
15 oz.	475 g	12 inches	30 cm
16 oz. (1 lb.)	500 g		
2 lb.	1 kg		

Oven temperatures

110°C	(225°F)	Gas ¼
120°C	(250°F)	Gas ½
140°C	(275°F)	Gas 1
150°C	(300°F)	Gas 2
160°C	(325°F)	Gas 3
180°C	(350°F)	Gas 4
190°C	(375°F)	Gas 5
200°C	(400°F)	Gas 6
220°C	(425°F)	Gas 7
230°C	(450°F)	Gas 8
240°C	(475°F)	Gas 9